Let's Draw

Jamaican Birds

Let's Draw Jamaican Birds

Guava Press, Blue Tang Ltd., Newmarket, ON L3X 2R6, Canada
ISBN 978-1-990380-23-5
Printed in India

Let's Draw

Jamaican Birds

Written by **Al Campbell**
Illustrated by **Sandra Macieira**

About this storybook

This is a storybook that's more than a storybook.

Enjoy reading, have fun and learn how to draw Jamaican birds.

(1) Trace each bird from the sketch on each even-numbered page.

(2) Draw each bird step-by-step.

(3) Colour each bird by following the coloured illustration example on each odd-numbered page.

What a fun way to learn about Jamaican birds!

Jade and Jamal live on the beautiful tropical island of Jamaica.

They are twins and they like to admire the nature around them.

Jade and Jamal also like to draw pictures.

One morning Jade saw her brother outside drawing pictures.

"What are you doing?" Jade asked Jamal.

"Drawing Jamaican birds," the boy replied. "Let's draw together!"

"OK, let's sketch each bird and colour it after," Jade suggested.

"We'll have lots of fun!" Jamal said. "Let's draw Jamaican birds!"

Doctor Bird

(Trochilus polytmus - male) ♂

"The doctor bird is our national bird," Jade said, "and it has many other names; like red-billed streamertail hummingbird, and ... "

"Swallow-tailed hummingbird," added Jamal, "long-tailed hummingbird, and scissor-tailed hummingbird. It's the most amazing hummingbird!"

Doctor Bird

(Trochilus polytmus - male) ♂

"The doctor bird's colour is bright green, with a black crown and a red beak," Jade noted, "while some even have yellow wing feathers."

"But do you know that only adult males have their most distinctive feature, the two long black streamertailed feathers?" Jamal asked.

Orangequit

(Euneornis campestris - male) ♂

"Which other amazing bird should we draw next?" Jade asked. "I hope it's another unique and exceptionally beautiful one."

"Orangequit is good," suggested Jamal, "and this bird is actually light blue in colour, with an orange-coloured tuft of feathers on its neck."

Orangequit

(Euneornis campestris - male) ♂

"Only the males are blue!" Jade noted. "Females have a lovely brown back and a deep grey crown."

"Orangequits are endemic to Jamaica," Jamal explained, "and guess what? They're the one and only member of the genus Euneornis."

Jamaican Owl

(*Asio grammicus*)

"Let's do the Jamaican owl next," Jade suggested, "or Patoo, as it's commonly called throughout the island."

"That sounds like the perfect choice!" Jamal agreed. "They're usually brown with different shades on their head, breast, body and wings."

Jamaican Owl

(*Asio grammicus*)

"Most of those are simply tiny specks of dark brown feathers that are dotted all over the Jamaican owl's body," Jade noted.

"Also, their entire breast area is light brown," Jamal said, "while the hornlike tufts of feathers atop their heads are usually dark brown."

Bananaquit

(Coereba flaveola - male) ♂

"Drawing birds is fun!" exclaimed Jade. "Let's draw as many as we can. What kind of Jamaican bird would you suggest next?"

"The bananaquit!" Jamal announced. "It's very tame and comes to our garden to feast on lots of sweet stuff. That's why it's called sugar bird."

Bananaquit

(Coereba flaveola - male) ♂

"The bananaquit is black above and yellow below," said Jade, "with white stripes near the eyes, as well as on its wings and body."

"And it loves to eat bananas!" Jamal added. "They'll use their long, sharp bills to easily pierce fruits or to suck nectar from flowers."

Jamaican Woodpecker

(Melanerpes radiolatus - male) ♂

"I know another bird that loves to eat," stated Jade, "and it makes lots of noise too; a constant and rapid tap-tap tapping sound and ... "

"I know, the Jamaican woodpecker!" Jamal said confidently. "It's so noisy with its wood tapping and other chirps, cackles, and calls."

Jamaican Woodpecker

(Melanerpes radiolatus - male) ♂

“They can have a white, grey, yellow or black head, neck, and breast, with a red crest of feathers atop the head like a crown,” stated Jade.

“The body, wings, and tail feathers are grey or black.” Jamal added. “They make sounds like this, ‘urp-urp-urp-urp’ or ‘urr-urr-urr-urr’.”

Yellow-shouldered Grassquit

(Loxipasser anoxanthus - male) ♂

"Probably one of the most commonly seen birds around Jamaica is the yellow-shouldered grassquit," said Jade. "We should draw it."

"The yellow-shouldered grassquit is grey or black, with lots of yellow feathers on its shoulders and wings," Jamal added. "I've seen many!"

Yellow-shouldered Grassquit

(Loxipasser anoxanthus - male) ♂

"Interestingly, both the males and females have the distinctive bright yellow-green shoulders," Jade observed. "That's unusual in birds."

"They too are endemic to Jamaica and they enjoy eating lots and lots of seeds," said Jamal. "They make many high-pitched buzzy sounds."

John Crow

(Cathartes aura)

"All the birds that we've drawn so far are small," Jade remarked. "We should draw a few big birds. Can you think of any big birds?"

"You're right!" Jamal agreed. "We should draw a few big-size birds, and the biggest bird that I can think of is the John Crow."

John Crow

(Cathartes aura)

"A John Crow is actually a turkey vulture," Jade explained. "The most distinctive feature they have is a bald red head and black feathers."

"They are carrion crows, which means they eat dead animals and because of that they are linked with a lot of bad things," said Jamal.

Brown Pelican

(Pelecanus occidentalis)

"What other big-size bird can you think of?" asked Jade. "There must be a few more that we would enjoy drawing together."

"The brown pelican is sort of big," Jamal responded. "Sometimes they are called Old Joe and they are mostly seen along the island's coast."

Brown Pelican

(Pelecanus occidentalis)

"The pelican is usually brown but some are grey or black," said Jade, "and its most distinctive feature is an enormous throat pouch."

"The throat pouch's colour varies from light brown to yellow or white," Jamal noted, "and they make grunting sounds like this, 'hrrraa-hrra'."

Jamaican Tody

(Todus todus - male) ♂

"Maybe we can go back to drawing small birds now?" said Jade. "Let's draw a very tiny bird! What's the tiniest bird you've ever seen?"

"The tiniest bird I've ever seen is the Jamaican tody," said Jamal. "They're commonly called Robin Redbreast and they're miniscule!"

Jamaican Tody

(Todus todus - male) ♂

"I've seen the Jamaican tody too!" announced Jade. "They're a brilliant green colour and sometimes they have white or yellow underparts."

"Most have a tuft of red feathers from below the beak to the top of the breast," said Jamal, "and they make fast scratchy 'zheh' sounds."

Jamaican Lizard-Cuckoo

(Coccyzus vetula - male) ♂

"And do you know another strikingly cute bird?" asked Jade.
"I do! It's not very small but it looks unbelievably amazing!"

"I bet you're talking about the Jamaican lizard-cuckoo," said Jamal.
"because it's long black and white tail is extremely impressive!"

Jamaican Lizard-Cuckoo

(Coccyzus vetula - male) ♂

"Yes!" Jade confirmed. "Jamaican lizard-cuckoos are brown or light grey from the crown all the way down the back, to the top of the tail."

"Below the neck are white feathers, and from the breast to near the tail can be pink or yellow," said Jamal. "Their voice is, 'k-k-k-kuh-kuh-kuh...'."

Yellow-billed Parrot

(Amazona collaria - male) ♂

"There're so many magnificent Jamaican birds, which type should we draw next?" asked Jade. "Should it be a spindalis, vireo, or parrot?"

"Let's draw a parrot!" said Jamal. "Let's draw a yellow-billed parrot with its brilliant green feathers and distinctive yellow beak."

Yellow-billed Parrot

(Amazona collaria - male) ♂

"The crown feathers are usually dark green or blue," Jade noted, "while red or yellow feathers form a sort of collar around its neck."

"Some also have white feathers from their beaks and up to around their eyes," said Jamal. "They sound like this, 'maa-weep' or 'mwah'."

Jamaican Mango

(Anthracothorax mango - male) ♂

"We've finished eleven illustrations," Jade said. "How about we draw one more to make it a total of twelve illustrations? One dozen in all!"

"That sounds good to me," agreed Jamal. "So let's make the final drawing be of the large but cute Jamaican mango hummingbird!"

Jamaican Mango

(Anthracothorax mango - male) ♂

"The upperparts of a Jamaican mango is usually dark green or brown," Jade said, "while below its back has purple outer tail feathers."

"The sides of the head and neck are also purple," noted Jamal, "and they usually like to make a sharp call that sounds like this, 'tsic'."

Jamaican Birds

"These are some very pretty pictures!" Jade remarked. "The birds are beautiful and our drawings are nice too. What do you think?"

"I like them all!" Jamal stated. "The sketches were good too. I wish we could have kept all the sketches."

Jamaican Birds

"Don't think about that," said Jade, "we had to do the sketches before we could go on to the colouring."

"That's true!" responded Jamal. "Come, let's have a look at our twelve wonderful illustrations of Jamaican birds!"

Jamaican Birds

"I think we captured the stunning beauty of Jamaican birds!" said Jade. "I like all our bird drawings! We did a good job!"

"Yes!" Jamal agreed. "Our island has many things in nature to admire. That's why we enjoyed drawing Jamaican birds!"